101 Celtic knotwork designs

101 Celtic knotwork designs

courtney davis

David & Charles

A DAVID & CHARLES BOOK

First published in 2004
Reprinted 2004

Distributed in North America
by F&W Publications, Inc.
4700 East Galbraith Road
Cincinnati, OH 45236
1-800-289-0963

A catalogue record for this book is available from the
British Library.

ISBN 0 7153 1666 4

Printed in Singapore by KHL Printing Co Pte Ltd
for David & Charles
Brunel House   Newton Abbot   Devon

Commissioning Editor Neil Baber
Desk Editor Sandra Pruski/Ame Verso
Art Editor Prudence Rogers
Designer Jodie Lystor
Production Controller Kelly Smith

I dedicate this book to the wings of angels.

My grateful thanks to Stephen Walker
and the staff at David & Charles for their
input on this book.

Visit our website at www.davidandcharles.co.uk

David & Charles books are available from all good
bookshops; alternatively you can contact our Orderline on
(0)1626 334555 or write to us at FREEPOST EX2110,
David & Charles Direct, Newton Abbot, TQ12 4ZZ
(no stamp required UK mainland).

contents

introduction by stephen walker

The Celtic art of Courtney Davis, along with other contemporary interpretations of Celtic design, is usually thought of in terms of its ancient and medieval prototypes. This is quite understandable because today these artworks, as well as jewellery, tattoo designs and Celtic crafts, are by their very subject and nature references to the past. But if this design history is to be understood as part of a living tradition, it is a mistake to ignore the evolution of the art in the more recent past.

An International Style

The Irish artist Henry O'Neill expressed the prevailing view of the 19th-century Celtic Revival in 1857, when he wrote in his book, *Illustrations of the Most Interesting of the Sculptured Crosses of Ancient Ireland*, 'I think that ancient Irish art was pagan, and was continued during the Christian period, just as the peculiar form of the Irish cross is pagan, or as the names of the months, or of the days of the week are pagan; these, and a great deal more of paganism, having continued, owing to the tenacity with which a people retain their general habits and ideas.' O'Neill was not himself pagan, as much of his writing contains a Christian piety that would refute such a suggestion; rather, he was expressing pride in a noble antiquity for Irish art. During the 19th-century Celtic Revival, much was said and written about native cultural survivals from 'pre-Christian' times, this term also meaning pre-Norman and before English domination. It must be remembered that at this time Ireland was reinventing itself. The trauma of famine and foreign rule was fresh. Many ancient Gaelic myths and legends were revived to serve the cause of a renewed sense of national identity and pride in the past.

O'Neill's opinions are still with us in popular folklore. He also wrote: 'In the fine arts the Ancient Irish were not influenced by the styles of other nations which had attained to great artistic excellence; the Irish invented a national style of art quite distinct from that of every other country, and in it they displayed a power of composition, colouring, and above all, of miraculous executive ability never equalled by any other people.' By the end of the 19th century scholars and archeologists alike had come to see the origins of Celtic art as a product of many cultural traditions, native as well as from outside.

The facts that the Romans never conquered Ireland or Scotland, and that the Saxon invasion of Britain did not reach much beyond England does not mean that the Celts had no cultural exchange with their neighbours, but the popular appeal of the concept that knotwork and the associated motifs of *Opus Hibernicum* were entirely unique and original examples of home-grown Celtic genius, had an emotional appeal that is difficult to abandon. The modern use of knotwork as an expression of cultural heritage has become so entrenched that it is often forgotten that knotwork was part of an international style during the Early Medieval period.

The Spread of Knotwork

Knotwork first appeared in Ireland, Scotland and northern England in the early 7th century, when Irish missionaries were evangelizing in Northumberland. The missionaries' main base was on the Isle of Iona, off the west coast of Scotland, and Picts in the north and Anglo-Saxons to the south quickly learned the scribal techniques of knotwork. The illumination of sacred books was spread, along with literacy and other forms of art and learning. This was a time of migrating ideas. Celtic monks, as well as those influenced by them, spread across northern Europe in the next several centuries while scholars from the continent flocked to Ireland, Iona, Lindisfarne and many other insular Celtic centres of learning.

While there is no direct historical data linking Adomnán, the 9th Abbot of Iona, to the Celtic artistic tradition of knotwork, the three most famous manuscripts known for their interlaced decoration, the *Book of Kells*, the *Book of Durrow* and the *Lindisfarne Gospels*, were all products of the community of faith and scholarship that would have been in place under Adomnán's leadership. The *Book of Durrow* might have been made during his lifetime (623–704), with the other two, and many more like them, made in the next century. During Adomnán's life artistic representations of knotwork became not only an international style, but also a new advance in artistic development for the Christian Celtic world.

Origins and Development

It is frequently misinterpreted and repeated that knotwork was a survival from an older Celtic-Druidic tradition, which was appropriated and renewed by Celtic Christians. This may be true of spiral motifs, which had a history in Celtic art going back for thousands of years, but not so for knotwork. It is true that ornamental and symbolic knotwork have been practiced by many cultures, some much older than the 7th century, but despite the beliefs of Henry O'Neill and others, knotwork burst forth on the insular Celtic scene quite suddenly.

Various sources have been suggested for the introduction of knotwork – one of the most interesting is that it came from Coptic Egypt, as there are many parallels between Celtic manuscripts and Coptic scribal techniques, materials and a very similar knotwork tradition. A 5th-century copy of the *Acts of the Apostles*, preserved in the Morgan Library in New York City, is seen by a number of scholars as the 'missing link' between the Celtic and Middle Eastern knotwork traditions.

However, any of the various knotwork traditions – Germanic, Mediterranean or Oriental – which could possibly have served as inspiration for the great Celtic interlace style, barely anticipate the mind-boggling complexity and imagination that very quickly developed after knotwork was adopted by the Christian Celts. Not only manuscript illumination, but also jewellery, liturgical metalwork, stone- and bone-carving, and quite likely crafts in other more perishable materials were writhing with knotwork and animal interlace. Knotwork was the most prevalent Celtic ornamental style from the 7th to 10th centuries. This style spread all across Europe during the Early Middle Ages, and although the Celtic style was not the only artistic source of the period, it was by far the most complex and sophisticated.

By the time of the Norman Invasion in the 11th century, knotwork was on the decline, but it continued in the Celtic world, primarily on the Gaelic fringe. Examples can be found in every century down to the present, although they get to be few and far between before the Celtic Revival of the 19th century. By the Later Middle Ages the style was strongest in the Scottish Highlands, where a style known as the Gaelic Revival continued a tradition of stone-carved interlace until the 16th century. Jewellery and weapons carried the tradition through the Jacobite period; the handles of dirks were still being carved with knotwork at the end of the 18th century. By this time the style had become a self-conscious statement of cultural and political identity.

The Modern Revival

Celtic art as a display of national and ethnic identity came into its own with the Irish Celtic Revival, beginning around 1840, when the collection and study of Irish antiquities began to be used as evidence of an advanced but lost culture. As a renewed sense of Irish identity was forged, reproductions of brooches from the golden age of Celtic art gained popularity. In 1851 the Dublin firm of Waterhouse and Co began to manufacture copies of the newly discovered 'Tara' Brooch. This splendid example of Celtic interlace ornament became itself a symbol of 'Celticness' along with round towers and wolfhounds. One of the first customers for the Waterhouse Tara Brooch was Queen Victoria, who purchased two at the Crystal Palace Exhibition of 1851.

The Celtic style again became international as the Revival spread to other Celtic countries, mainly Scotland and the Isle of Man, but also through the Celtic diaspora around the world. Knotwork and animal interlace were the most common and popular Celtic design elements, as they continue to be to this day. Designs directly derivative of ancient models gradually gave way to newly created designs, inspired by antique examples but showing creativity and adaptation by new generations of artists. By the 1890s the Celtic Revival had influenced the Arts and Crafts and Art Nouveau movements.

Prior to this time, Celtic Revival designs had largely been an imitation of the ancient art. When new artists and designers began to experiment with knotwork and the other elements of Celtic art, several of the most radical changes occurred in the style in over a thousand years. Many artists broke from the faithful reproduction of models such as the *Book of Kells*, and began to treat the graphic and sculptural forms of interlace in a fresh, modern approach.

Some kept the strict conventions of over-under alternations and endless paths of the cord, but others treated designs as impressionistic references to the Celtic style, seeking the 'feel' of Celtic design without being too fussy about the ornamental grammar.

The Meaning of Knotwork

The occasional panels of knotwork that survive on medieval buildings as lintels above doors may hold a clue to medieval magical or symbolic purposes for carved knotwork. A doorway is both a barrier and an entry; real knots bind and secure. The use of symbolic knots at a threshold can be interpreted as a charm for strength and security and protection against evil. A real knot consists of tied rope or cord that naturally has two ends. A drawn or carved knot with no end may hope to confuse and ensnare the devil by compelling the evil one to follow the path, hopelessly searching for its start and end.

However, the majority of old knotwork that survives was part of a more elaborate message. The *Book of Durrow*, for instance, is loaded with knotwork, but it is not about knotwork; like the *Book of Kells* and the *Lindisfarne Gospels*, it is about the word of God. The knotwork, symbolic or decorative, exists to glorify the Gospels. In the same way the wonderful penannular brooches of the same period were highly embellished with knotwork, but their form was the conventional form of a brooch.

All this began to change when designers such as Archibald Knox and Alexander Ritchie started to make brooches in the form of knots, and knotwork more frequently became the subject of designs, rather than secondary to other messages or purposes. When these modern Celtic designers began to take elements such as single knots and make these the focus of designs, or even to make a single knot the entire object, this was a profoundly creative act. Knots and details were beginning, more often, to take on lives of their own as stand-alone statements.

Knots as Symbols

There is no key to specific meanings for ancient knotwork, yet there are plenty of examples of knots-as-symbols in modern Celtic art. The idea of continued and consistent ancient purpose can be understood better, and perhaps dismissed, if we set aside the 'from-the-*Book-of-Kells*' tag line that has so frequently been used in the description of modern Celtic art. Knotwork existed in other cultures for many centuries before it arrived on Celtic shores, so that symbolism which emerges in our own time may have its roots in the distant past, and it may also evolve new messages with the journey through time.

The most reliable medieval symbolic use of knotwork is as a sign of the cross. There are many examples of cross-shaped knots as well as knots that very subtly conceal crosses in the space between the ribbons of the knotwork. Knots with specific names, intended as signs for certain ideas are actually very rare. The triquetra knot, also called the Trinity knot, is the most well-known. In Christian use this very attractive knot has been used as a reference to the Father, Son and Holy Spirit. It is very rare to see this knot in medieval work displayed as the central symbol of a design in the same context as a cross would be shown. For this reason some have argued that this meaning is without evidence – like the subtler cross knots, it is easy to imagine the repeated use of triquetra knots by prayerful monks as meaningful, but the triquetra has only been used as a Trinity symbol from the 19th century.

The notion of knots with pat definitions like 'love', 'eternity' or 'purity', and as charms for strength, courage or health is something the historian would dismiss as silly. Sadly, some marketers of Celtic giftware seem to have simply matched up knots with saleable sentiments, which certainly does amount to a kind of bogus cultural pollution. But why can't a knot be a symbol of love or some other message? Some knots make sense as representations of certain ideas: for example, the Josephine's knot or granny knot links together separate individual strands, and has been called a lover's knot since it represents joining together. Likewise, heart-shaped knots can be used as an expression of love; and why not? The use of the heart shape as a sign of love is a later symbol that certainly would not have been in use during the time of the *Book of Kells*, but expansion of the vocabulary of symbolic knotwork to include heart knots shows that the tradition is a living and evolving process.

The Continuum of Knotwork

The 20th-century Scottish art teacher George Bain observed in his book, *Celtic Art: the Methods of Construction*, that endless paths were the ideal in Celtic knotwork, and that in many cases very elaborate designs were made that consisted of a single strand. It has been a common interpretation of Bain's comments that 'continuum' was an important message of knotwork. When it is realized that modern use of this art form is so often done as a reference to heritage and historical interests, the message of continuum makes perfect sense. Any knot that has no beginning or end may be seen as an 'eternity' knot. Eternal what? Life, love and faith – all strike an emotional chord. Knotwork can be seen as a metaphor for the interconnectedness of life. This is not the kind of statement that can be sourced and footnoted – it is the intuitive symbolism of a living and evolving art form.

designs
in stone

Part of a collection of late 7th- or early 8th-century stone fragments in Reculver,
Kent, regarded as among the best examples of Anglo-Saxon sculpture. *Canterbury
Cathedral, Kent, England*

A simple knotwork pattern from the late 9th- or early 10th-century Conbelin cross slab.
Margam Abbey Museum, West Glamorgan, Wales

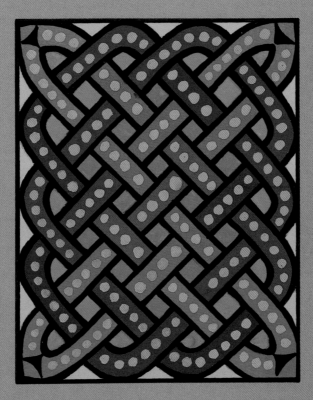

Continuous circular knotwork design from a stone carved bossed disc on the 9th-century Shandwick Stone. *Shandwick, Ross and Cromarty, Scotland*

designs in stone

This nicely shaped design is from a panel in the 9th-century Glamis cross slab. *Glamis, Angus, Scotland*

A knotwork disc consisting of four interwoven bands from the 9th-century Glamis cross slab. *Glamis, Angus, Scotland*

A section of the 9th-century Aberlemno cross slab. *Aberlemno, Angus, Scotland*

A fine example of a continuous thread from the 9th-century Hilton of Cadbol cross slab.
Royal Museum of Scotland, Edinburgh, Scotland

Triangular knotwork panel from the 9th-century Straithmartin stone cross.
Straithmartin, Angus, Scotland

nine

A continuous thread from the 9th-century Hilton of Cadbol cross slab. *Royal Museum of Scotland, Edinburgh, Scotland*

ten

Simple knotwork from the late 8th-century Ulbster cross slab. *Ulbster, Caithness, Scotland*

eleven

Knotwork from the late 8th-century Ulbster cross slab. *Ulbster, Caithness, Scotland*

twelve

One of the panels from the highly decorative 8th-century Nigg Stone, which is a superb blend of high and low decorative carving. *Nigg, Ross and Cromarty, Scotland*

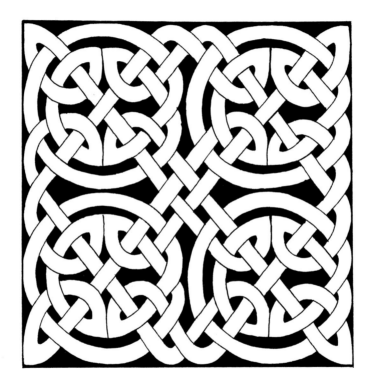

Fine knotwork design panels from the mid 8th-century Nigg Stone. *Nigg, Ross and Cromarty, Scotland*

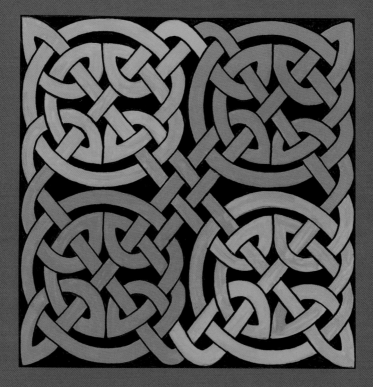

A highly intricate design from the mid 8th-century St Madoes cross slab, which is housed within a protective box and rarely seen. *St Madoes, Perthshire, Scotland*

fifteen

A simple design taken from one of the six 11th-century high crosses at Kilfenora.
Kilfenora, Co Clare, Ireland

A knotwork design from one of the six stone crosses at Kilfenora from around the 11th century. *Kilfenora, Co Clare, Ireland*

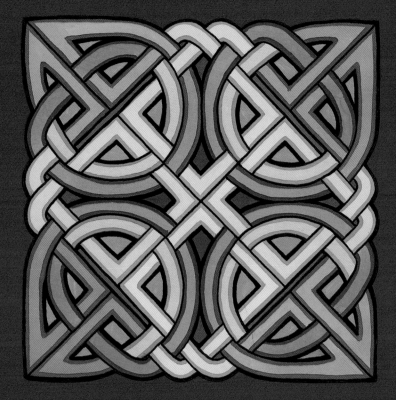

Section of the 9th-century Glamis Manse cross, probably the earliest surviving cross slab.
Glamis, Angus, Scotland

Section of the 9th-century Aberlemno cross slab. *Aberlemno, Angus, Scotland*

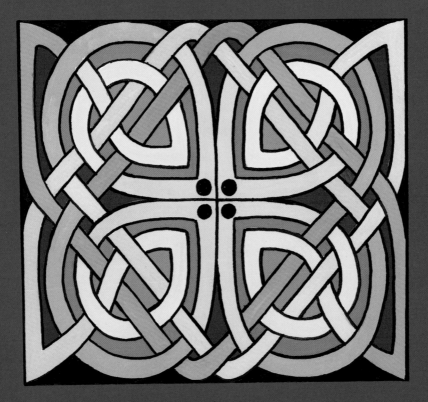

nineteen

Section from the 9th-century Aberlemno cross slab. The relief is so high that the central cross, from which the design here is taken, looks almost freestanding. *Aberlemno, Angus, Scotland*

designs in stone

Section from the central cross of the 9th-century Aberlemno cross slab. *Aberlemno, Angus, Scotland*

Design on a pillar of the 9th-century St Peter's church. *Britford, Wiltshire, England*

twenty-two

Knotwork panel design of a late 8th-century Anglo-Saxon frieze at St Hardulph's church.
Breedon-on-the-Hill, Leicestershire, England

twenty-three

This panel from the mid 8th-century Rossie Priory cross slab is sometimes called a 'page in stone', as it is thought to represent a page of a book. *Rossie Priory, Tayside, Scotland*

Based on a design on the late 8th-century Canna Cross shaft. *Canna, Hebrides, Scotland*

Based on a design on the late 8th-century Canna cross shaft. *Canna, Hebrides, Scotland*

An unusual staggered design from a 10th-century cross shaft. *Monasterboice, Co Louth, Ireland*

twenty-seven

An intricate, though not continuous, thread from an 8th-century cross shaft. *Golden Grove, Carmarthenshire, Wales*

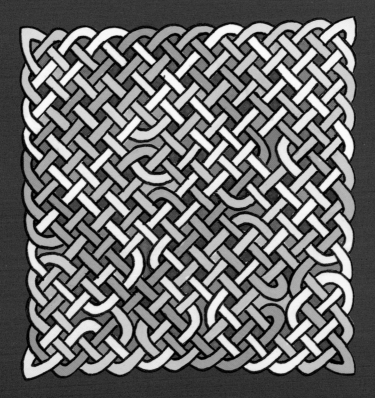

designs in metalwork

twenty-eight

Terminal from an 8th-century chip-carved penannular brooch which was part of a hoard discovered in 1868. *Royal Museum of Scotland, Edinburgh, Scotland*

twenty-nine

Irish open bronze mount with a central S motif from around 100BC–100AD. *National Museum of Ireland, Dublin, Ireland*

Design from a panel on a 9th-century Oseberg harness mount. *Universitetets Oldsaksamling, Oslo, Norway*

Interlaced rectangular panel from a hinged shrine mount from the 8th or 9th centuries.
National Museum of Ireland, Dublin, Ireland

designs in metalwork

A 9th-century Irish roundel that was originally part of a harness mount, found in a hoard of Viking loot in Norway. *Universitetets Oldsaksamling, Oslo, Norway*

thirty-three

Adaptation of a panel from the magnificent early 8th-century Ardagh Chalice. *National Museum of Ireland, Dublin, Ireland*

designs in metalwork

Roundel from a silver penannular brooch from the 8th century. *Royal Museum of Scotland, Edinburgh, Scotland*

thirty-five

Section of knotwork from St Patrick's Bell Shrine from the 11th century. Many of the motifs of the cast bronze shrine are in the Viking Urnes style. *National Museum of Ireland, Dublin, Ireland*

Taken from a chip-carved panel on a set of 8th-century conjoined silver-gilt pins. *British Museum, London, England*

Design from an 8th–9th-century Anglo-Saxon bronze-gilt bookmount. *National Museum of Ireland, Dublin, Ireland*

Strap end showing the Scandinavian Borre/Jelling style influence on 9th–10th-century knotwork. A similar pattern can be seen on the Gosforth Cross in Cumberland. *Yorkshire Museum, York, England*

Design taken from a 15th-century leather book satchel for the 9th-century Book of Armagh. *National Museum of Ireland, Dublin, Ireland*

Knotwork design on an 8th-century writing tablet made from bone and copper alloy.
British Museum, London, England

The 11th-century Urnes style Trondheim Pin is a fine example of Viking bone-working.
Vitenskapsmuseel, Trondheim, Norway

designs in illuminated manuscripts

FORCY~CWO

A small section of the Symbol of St Matthew from the late 7th-century Echternach Gospels. *Bibliothéque Nationale, Paris, France*

forty-three

The terminal end of a large initial from the opening page of Collectio canonum, an early 8th-century manuscript. *Cologne Cathedral Library, Cologne, Germany*

Knotwork panel from the opening page of Collectio canonum from the early 8th-century manuscript Dombibliothek Cod 213. *Cologne Cathedral Library, Cologne, Germany*

Forty-five

Section from the cross-shaped panel surrounding the Portrait of Matthew in the early 8th-century Trier Gospels. *Bibliothéque Nationale, Paris, France*

forty-six

An adapted section from the portrait of Matthew from the early 8th-century Trier Gospels. Some of the illumination has many similarities to the manuscripts of Durham and Echternach of the same period. *Bibliothéque Nationale, Paris, France*

forty-seven

Tail of an initial letter of St. John's Gospel from the 7th-century Durham Gospels.
Durham Cathedral Library, Durham, England

forty-eight

Early 8th-century knotwork panel taken from Cassiodorus's Commentary on the Psalms.
Durham Cathedral Library, Durham, England

forty-nine

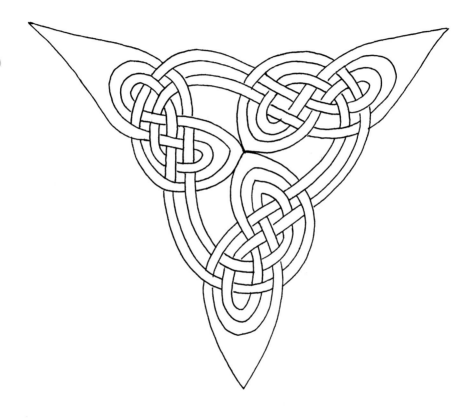

Triquetra design symbolizing the Trinity from the early 8th-century Lindisfarne Gospels.
British Library, London, England

Fifty

Section of knotwork that forms part of a border surrounding the portrait of David from the 8th-century Durham Gospels. *Durham Cathedral Library, Durham, England*

fifty-one

Section of a border panel from the 8th-century Durham Gospels that surrounds the portrait of David from Cassiodorus's Commentary on the Psalms. *Durham Cathedral Library, Durham, England*

fifty-two

Knotwork design from the Royal Bible, dated to the mid 9th-century and produced in Canterbury. The design is not a true continuous knot and consists of five separate knots entwined. *British Museum, London, England*

fifty-three

Adapted from the border of a cross carpet, or fully illuminated, page in the Lichfield Gospels (also known as the Gospel of Chad) from around 730. *Lichfield Cathedral Library, Staffordshire, England*

Adapted from the border of a cross carpet page in the Lichfield Gospels (also known as the Gospel of Chad) from around 730. The manuscript probably originated from Northumbria. *Lichfield Cathedral Library, Staffordshire, England*

A slightly altered design taken from an initial in the late 7th-century Echternach Gospels. *Bibliothéque Nationale, Paris, France*

fifty-six

Knotwork design from the late 7th-century Book of Durrow, which is the earliest surviving fully illuminated Gospel book. *Trinity College, Dublin, Ireland*

fifty seven

Cross panel design from the late 7th-century Book of Durrow, thought to have been produced in a Columban monastery – although whether it was in Ireland, Iona or Northumbria is uncertain. *Trinity College, Dublin, Ireland*

fifty-eight

Knotwork design from the late 7th-century Book of Durrow, which may have been executed by Eadfrith, the same artist who created the Lindisfarne Gospels. *Trinity College, Dublin, Ireland*

fifty-nine

Knotwork design from the late 7th-century Book of Durrow, which is the earliest surviving fully illuminated Gospel book. *Trinity College, Dublin, Ireland*

sixty

Knotwork panel design from the late 7th-century Book of Durrow. *Trinity College, Dublin, Ireland*

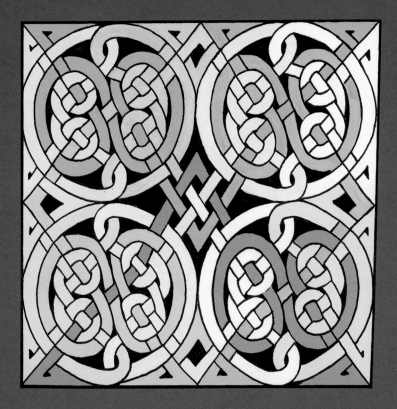

sixty-one

Triple-banded knotwork design from the Liber Generationis page of the 9th-century illuminated masterpiece, the Book of Kells. *Trinity College, Dublin, Ireland*

sixty-two

Central border design in the 9th-century Book of Kells. *Trinity College, Dublin, Ireland*

sixty–three

Six connecting petals from the 9th-century Book of Kells, the most famous of all the insular manuscripts and the pinnacle of Celtic draughtsmanship. *Trinity College, Dublin, Ireland*

sixty-four

This knotwork panel from the 9th-century Book of Kells is adapted from a border surrounding an eight-circled cross, where it is used four times. A lion's head sits on each corner of the original. *Trinity College, Dublin, Ireland*

sixty–five

This knotwork cross design separates two large spiral discs at the beginning of St John's Gospel in the 9th-century Book of Kells. *Trinity College, Dublin, Ireland*

Central border design in the 9th-century Book of Kells. *Trinity College, Dublin, Ireland*

sixty~seven

A knotwork border design from the late 7th-century Book of Durrow adapted into a circle. *Trinity College, Dublin, Ireland*

sixty-eight

A border design from the late 7th-century Book of Durrow adapted into a knotwork panel. *Trinity College, Dublin, Ireland*

sixty-nine

An adapted border from the late 7th-century Book of Durrow. *Trinity College, Dublin, Ireland*

seventy

An interlaced panel from the late 7th-century Book of Durrow. *Trinity College, Dublin, Ireland*

seventy-one

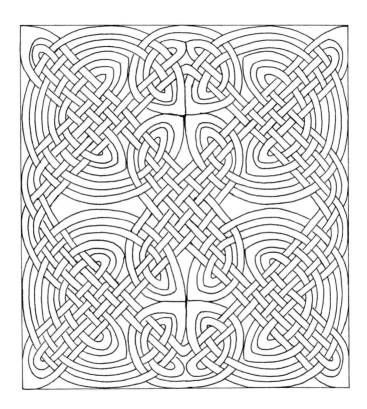

A panel design from the Lindisfarne Gospels, thought to have been created by Eadfrith, who became Bishop of Lindisfarne in 1688. *British Library, London, England*

seventy~two

A panel design from the Lindisfarne Gospels, which is dedicated to St Cuthbert and is thought to have actually been written and illuminated by Eadfrith in the late 7th century for his own use. *British Library, London, England*

seventy~three

Design from an initial in the 7th-century Echternach Gospels. *Bibliothéque Nationale, Paris, France*

seventy-four

A panel from an initial in the 7th-century Echternach Gospels, which is thought to have been sent as a gift from Lindisfarne to St Willibrod's new monastery in Echternach (Luxembourg). *Bibliothéque Nationale, Paris, France*

designs in illuminated manuscripts

An interlaced pattern from the late 7th-century Lindisfarne Gospels. *British Library,
London, England*

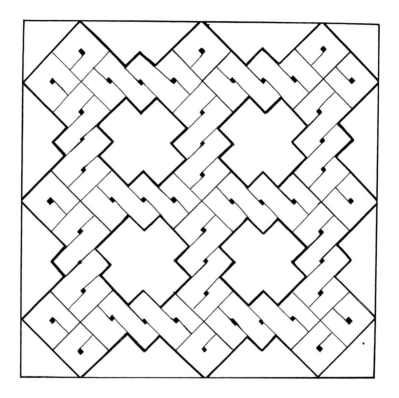

seventy-six

A straight interlaced panel from the late 7th-century Book of Durrow. *Trinity College, Dublin, Ireland*

seventy~seven

Section from the beginning of St John's Gospel from the 9th-century Bible of Charles the Bald. *Bibliothéque Nationale, Paris, France*

seventy-eight

Slightly altered section from the beginning of St John's Gospel from the 9th-century Bible of Charles the Bald. *Bibliothéque Nationale, Paris, France*

seventy–nine

Design from the terminal of a large initial from St Matthew's Gospel from the 9th-century Saint-Martin-des-Champs Gospels. *Bibliothéque de l'Arsenal, Paris, France*

designs in illuminated manuscripts

Border design from the 10th-century Bible of the Year 960 Omega. *Collegiate Church of San Isidoro, León, Spain*

eighty~one

In the 9th century spirals began to disappear in illumination, and intricate knotwork patterns became simplified. This decal is from the beginning of St John's Gospel from the Bible of Charles the Bald. *Bibliothéque Nationale, Paris, France*

designs in illuminated manuscripts

There was a resurgence of interest in Celtic design during the 19th century. This design comes from a book cover designed by the English binders Robert Riviere and Son.

Adapted Celtic design from a 19th-century book cover by the English binders
F Sangorski and G Sutcliff.

modern
designs

eighty-four

Design created from two bands of interlace.

This is similar to design 84, but the centre now joins the two bands together.

Two separate bands of interlace forming a cross.

This is similar to design 86, but the centre now draws in and makes a continuous thread.

Interlace star design from a single thread.

Interlace star design forming a cross at the centre.

The triquetra symbolizes the Trinity, although it was originally thought to symbolize the ancient Celtic Triple Goddess.

ninety~one

Design based on a terminal from an initial in the 7th-century Echternach Gospels and then doubled up.

An adapted interlace pattern with origins in the Lindisfarne Gospels.

ninety-three

Two terminal designs based on a joined and corrected initial in the 7th-century
Echternach Gospels.

Like the Gordian knot cut by Alexander the Great, in Celtic tradition the continuous knot binds the soul to the world until the thread is broken and the soul is released to begin its spiritual journey.

Spirals were the first patterns to be used by Celtic scribes, but the use of interlace, which came shortly after in books such as the Durham Gospels, carried on long after spirals were discarded.

This is a squared version of design 95.

ninety~seven

Taken from the corner of a border in the Lindisfarne Gospels, this design was doubled up and slightly altered to fit to a continuous thread.

To the early Celts the skull was believed to be both a source of power and a trophy. The sacred use of a blessed or holy skull was preserved in several holy wells in Britain and Ireland as late as the 18th century.

ninety~nine

A knotwork panel built up from a single terminal of an initial in the early 8th-century
Collectio canonum.

one hundred

Illuminated books and decorated stone crosses were a way of showing the wonder of the Word of God to a population who could not read for themselves. Like a mandala, they could be used to meditate upon the message in the Gospels.

one hundred and one

Design formed by repeating a triquetra, the symbol of the Trinity, from the late 7th-century Lindisfarne Gospels.